About the author...

Before locking herself away in a small room to write Survivor's Guides, Jeanette Baker worked for several teenage magazines including *Just Seventeen*, *LOOKS*, *more!* and finally *MIZZ* where she was editor. She lives in London with her husband Simon who also happens to be her best friend. Despite being far too old for it she's still a sucker for wild girls' nights out (or in) with her fantastic mates who never fail to make her laugh, and put up with her despite her pathetic staying power.

With many thanks to Andrew Dean and the members of Finchley Youth Theatre for their invaluable words of wisdom.

About the illustrator...

Polly Dunbar is 21 years old and has recently graduated from Brighton Art School. Her friends have always been a great inspiration and much of her material comes directly from real life. This has sometimes got her into trouble with them but luckily, she says, they are still great mates and give as good as they get.

LOVE ETC   SCHOOL   FAMILIES

J302.34

Contents...

Friends — who needs them?

We all need friends

I f you've been let down by a friend recently or your mates are just getting on your nerves, you may feel like saying 'Get lost!' to the lot of them and looking around for some new ones. Fair enough, but before you decide that's definitely what you're going to do, please take some time to consider the following points:

• Finding new friends isn't always easy. Unfortunately, there isn't a mail order catalogue that delivers funny, reliable, popular mates within 48-hours or your money back.

• If friendship were that easy, this would be a very short book indeed. In fact, it would be a pamphlet or a Post-it note.

"Dan... your new friends are here!"

• If you ditch this lot of friends and find some new ones, sooner or later they're probably going to get on your nerves or let you down too. That's life.

OK, so you feel like killing your mates, or you may wish that you'd never set eyes on them in the first place. In fact, who needs friends anyway? You've got the telly, and the cat, and chips. But before you give up on your friends completely, just take a minute to imagine what life would be like without them.

• Who would you share your jokes with?
• Who would spend hours knocking about with you?
• Who would help you get ready for that big night out?

- Who could you hang around with?
- Who else can you talk to about almost everything, knowing that they'll understand?

'I know you understand.'

Tell me about it

'Friends come in useful on Valentine's Day – most of the people I know got their friends to send them cards so that they didn't look sad.' **Peter, 13**

'My friends and I help each other out with our school work.' **Lucy, 12**

'Cheers mate!'

'You need your friends when you're feeling upset or just down in the dumps about something.' **Natalie, 13**

'Your friends are important when you want to talk to someone about anything and everything, and share your secrets with them.'
Louise, 14

'You know Sam, you're the only one who really listens to me.'

Tell me about it

'Friends should be the people you talk to when you can't talk to anyone else.' **Toby, 11**

'Sometimes you need a friend who's a bit older who can give you advice and help you out because they've already been through it.' **Ben, 12**

The great thing about friends is that, unlike parents, teachers and brothers and sisters, they're usually going through the same kind of experiences and emotions as you at pretty much the same time, so who better to talk through your problems with? They may not have all the answers, but if they're really good friends they'll make the effort to find someone else who does.

Making friendship work isn't always going to be easy, but if you crack it, these could be some of the most important relationships you'll ever have in your life. And let's face it, falling out with your mates isn't exactly a bundle of laughs is it? That's why if you've got friendship problems at the moment, you could do a lot worse than check out this Survivor's Guide, because if you're prepared to put some effort into your friendships, it should result in you and your mates making it through the good times and the bad times.

Spot the true friend

The only trouble with really good friends is that when you've known them for ages and things are going fine, it can be easy to take them for granted. It's therefore worth reminding yourself every now and then exactly what a true friend is supposed to be.

How to spot a 'true' friend

This rare species can initially be difficult to detect. They could be male or female, short or tall, in fact you won't necessarily recognize them just by their appearance. You may think you've found one, but before you can be absolutely sure it will be necessary to study their behaviour in their natural habitat over a fairly long period of time. In order to help you track down and keep hold of a true friend, read the following list of identifiable qualities.

'My goodness, we have so much in common.'

'What kind of friend are you?'

A true friend is:

- someone who shares the good times and the bad
- someone who you can talk to about pretty much everything
- someone who you know will keep a secret
- someone who will stick with you when the going gets tough
- someone who you can have a laugh with
- someone who you know will be loyal to the end

Nancy found her imaginary friend rather unsupportive.

And another thing...

True friends don't grow on trees and if you want some for yourself then you've got to make the effort to be a true friend back. Yep, this is a two-way street thing, because no matter how fantastic your mates are, they aren't going to hang around for long if they don't get anything back from you. So if you're wondering why you keep meeting really great people who then mysteriously stop calling you, it may be worth thinking about what kind of friend you are.

Fake friends grow on trees.

Are you a great mate?

The good friend/bad friend quiz

Why not grab some paper and a pen, then try this quiz. Find out the truth about yourself.

1 If you were at a party and you saw your best mate's boyfriend/girlfriend snogging someone else in the kitchen, would you:

a Say nothing. You might have got it wrong and you don't want to upset your mate unnecessarily.

b Tell your friend that you're worried you may have seen something going on and suggest that he/she talks to their boyfriend/girlfriend about it.

c Pretend you didn't see a thing – it's none of your business and you don't want to get caught in the middle.

2 If any of your mates were getting really behind with their homework and revision in one particular subject at school, would you:

a Find out exactly what work they have missed and then let them copy yours.

b Ask them if they would like some help with the work and if you can't help suggest they talk to their year head about it.

c Tell them not to get stressed about it – there are plenty of other subjects to work on and you could both skip any difficult lessons and go to town together instead.

'I saw your boyfriend kissing the kitchen fridge.'

3 If any of your friends bought some new clothes that looked terrible on them, would you:

a Say they look great because you know they like the outfit and you wouldn't want to hurt their feelings.

b Say something like, 'I'm not sure those particular clothes really suit you', and suggest they swap them for something else.

c Laugh like a drain when they try them on, and tell them they'd be mad to go out in public looking like that.

4 If one of your mates was having a nightmare time at home with brothers and sisters getting on their nerves and parents giving them a hard time, would you:

a Encourage them to come over to your house as much as possible just to get away from it all.

b Suggest that they sit down with their mum or dad and explain that the arguing is really upsetting them and that they'd like to know if there's anything they can do to help the situation.

c Tell them they should get out more so that they have something else to talk about.

5 If one of your mates wanted you to organize something for their birthday, would you:

a Arrange an evening for the two of you including all their favourite things – videos/chocolate/pizza/Tomb Raider, etc.
b Get together with their other mates and family and work out with everyone how to arrange the perfect night.
c Invite them along to a party you were going to anyway on the night of their birthday.

Now count up whether you scored mostly A's, B's or C's and look over the page for some insight and advice.

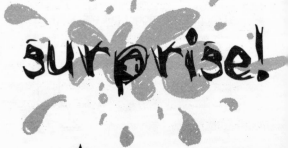

surprise!

Mostly A's

Ever wondered why it seems as though you're always bending over backwards to help out your mates, and yet they never seem to be there for you when you need them? This is probably because as well as being a great mate, you can also be a bit of a push-over when it comes to friendship, and although your heart is in the right place, you may be guilty of over-protecting or smothering your mates with kindness. Believe it or not, this can do more harm than good. How? Well, ask yourself this: are your mates constantly taking advantage of you and always asking for favours and help? Do you sometimes wish they'd ask how you were or what you wanted to do for a change? If the answer's 'Yes', then you need to remind yourself that truly good friends should be honest with each other – even if that means telling them that they're getting on your nerves/being stupid/taking the mick. This doesn't mean you have to yell at them every time they rub you up the wrong way, and when you do confront them you don't have to be too blunt and to the point. Just try saying how you really feel, even if it's not what your friend may want to hear. If he/she listens and accepts it, then you know that you're well on the way to developing a lifelong friendship.

Mostly B's

Let's face it, if there was a Friends Olympics, you'd be gold medal material. You certainly seem to have this friendship thing cracked because you know when to listen, when to talk and when to tell it like it is. Without losing your identity, you've managed to combine honesty and understanding in your friendships, which is why you're really appreciated by your mates – even if they don't always show it. The main thing for you to remember now is that friendship should always be about give and take, and it shouldn't always be you who is doing the giving. Don't get so bogged down in other people's problems that you wear yourself down, and if you need some help from your friends, don't be afraid to ask – you'll probably find that they're delighted to pay back some of the favours they owe you.

Jonathan always knew what to do in a crisis.

great mate

Mostly C's

Erm, excuse me, is there any chance you could take a moment to read this very important message please?

> IF YOU DON'T START SHOWING A BIT OF CONSIDERATION FOR OTHERS, AND STOP THINKING ABOUT YOURSELF THE WHOLE TIME, YOU WILL END UP AS A TOTAL NORMAN-NO-MATES. THANK YOU.

Have you ever wondered why your so-called mates don't seem to stick around for too long?
Probably not, because when they do disappear you don't seem to have any trouble attracting new mates – after all, you're the life and soul of the party, and everyone knows they'll have a good time if they hang out with you. But sooner or later, you may run out of new mates – especially the type who always do what you say, and run around after you – and that's when the 'N.N.M' syndrome will kick in.

You may be great for a laugh, but there's a lot more to friendship than just sharing the good times. If your mates don't see you for dust when times are hard, how can you expect them to be there for you when you're going through a rough patch? It can be difficult, and sometimes downright depressing being around unhappy people, but the sad fact is that life isn't going to be one long party and you and your friends will have to go through some tough times. So instead of constantly worrying about your favourite subject, i.e. 'You', try taking the time to look a little more closely at what your friends are going through and think about how you could help them for a change. You may even discover that it makes you feel better knowing that you've helped.

'You think you've got problems! It isn't easy looking this good, you know.'

Best ears for listening

Best laugh

Best shoulder to cry on

Best trainers!

what is a best friend?

Have you got a 'best' friend, and if you have, what exactly did this friend do to earn that prestigious title? Is a best friend the one who buys you the best birthday present? Or is a best friend the best-looking, best-dressed person you know? Probably not. In reality, the term 'best friend' will often mean totally different things to different people.

A best friend is:

Tell me about it

'Someone who, even if someone better or cooler comes along, won't desert you.' **Richard, 13**

'A best friend will always stick up for you, even if it puts them in a difficult position.' **Belinda, 15**

'Someone you can be 100 per cent honest with.' **Rebecca, 13**

'Hold still, something nasty landed on your hair.'

24

'Will you still be my friend if I wear smelly trainers on my head?'

'A best friend won't give you a hard time about the way you look or what you wear, they just let you be yourself.' **Sean, 13**

'I think you make your best friends at senior school because when you're at primary school people just want to be your friend if you look a certain way, or have cool things, whereas when you get to senior school you care more about the person inside.' **Luke, 14**

'When you're having a fall out with your other friends, your best friend will stand by you no matter what.' **Susie, 14**

top friend

Best friends are great because:

- they know everything about you, and you know everything about them
- they always know how to cheer you up
- you don't have to explain why you're feeling miserable, they just know
- they share loads of your best memories
- they'll happily lend you clothes/records/books/games, and you trust them with yours too
- they're great to confide in if you've got a secret

Tell me about it

'With a best friend you don't have to like exactly the same things, you can still be friends and agree to disagree on some things.'
Leah, 14

'A best friend should know the difference between teasing and mucking about and what's nasty and hurtful.' **Sam, 12**

'When you're best friends with someone you help each other out and forgive each other if you do something wrong.' **Tom, 13**

brilliant!

Posse
power

Of course not everybody has just one best friend and there's nothing wrong with you if you don't. Being part of a group of close mates, as opposed to having just one best friend, can have its uses too:

Tell me about it

'You feel safer when you hang out as a group – there's more people to stick up for you.' **Tamara, 13**

'You can have more of a laugh with a whole group of you – when you tell a joke and there's only one person there to laugh it's not quite the same is it?' **Michael, 14**

'There are quite a few things that are more of a laugh when there's a group of you, like going swimming or going to the cinema.' **Shamilla, 12**

Groups of mates are great because:

• you're not always unloading all your troubles on to one set of shoulders

• the bigger the group of friends, the more advice you will get when trying to tackle a problem because hopefully they'll come up with different suggestions between them

• you don't get totally sick of each other because you can divide your time between different friends

• you'll never be short of someone to hang out with

• if your group of mates is made up of boys and girls, you will get a different perspective on things

Katie liked to share her problems.

On the other hand, although lots of the time it can be a real laugh hanging out with a group of mates, make sure you don't neglect your individual friendships, because Posse Power can have its disadvantages:

Tell me about it

'If you're part of a group of friends with an odd number of people in it, you can end up feeling left out if you're the one who ends up not having anyone to sit next to in class or pair up with for games.'
Sebastian, 12

'When we first went to secondary school my best mate and I hung around in a big group which was sometimes pretty annoying because as soon as two people in the group fell out you had to decide whose side you were going to be on.' **Lorraine, 14**

'It's horrible if you fall out with the leader of the group because they make sure that everyone else turns against you.'
Naomi, 12

'Forgive me, oh mighty posse leader.'

Friendship rescue

They may be your mates, but that won't necessarily stop you from falling out with each other every now and then, for all sorts of reasons.

Tell me about it

'If you're off school sick for a day, sometimes you come back to find that your supposed best friend has gone off with other people and has decided she's not your friend any more.' **Saskia, 13**

'When you're younger you fall out with people if you don't want to join in with their games.' **Ellie, 11**

'A friend might say something that doesn't seem that bad to them, but you might find it really painful and upsetting. When that happens you go home and think about it all night and it can be really upsetting.' **Ali, 13**

'Gosh, your new dress makes me look really thin.'

'I'll forgive you but I won't forget.'

'My friendship with a girl who I've known ever since nursery school was nearly broken up because she had an argument with another girl who was also my friend. I ended up being caught in the middle – if I spoke to one of them the other one would go all huffy.' **Caroline, 12**

'If you break up with a friend and have an argument, even if they apologize to you sometimes it's still really hard not to carry on thinking about what they did and how they let you down.' **Andrew, 13**

Nobody likes arguing or falling out with their mates, and in an ideal world you wouldn't have anything to fall out about. But no matter how well you get on with your friends, or how understanding you all are, there will be times when you want to kill each other. Obviously when this happens it would be better if you didn't resort to violence or death – it's painful, messy, and there's an awful lot of explaining to do if you get caught trying to get rid of the body. Instead, you could take the mature approach and rather than just turning your back on friendship in times of trouble, you could confront the problems head on and deal with them.

'So, Michael, what do you think, would your body fit in here or would you prefer something more comfortable?'

Problem:

Developing doormat syndrome

'I hate arguing with any one, especially friends, which means that even when they really get on my nerves, or treat me badly, I won't stand up to them and tell them how I feel. I suppose I'm scared of how they'll react if I say anything, and I'm worried that they'll end up hating me and I won't have any friends at all. So how do I stop getting walked all over by mates who know I won't stand up to them?'

'Excuse me, that rather hurts.'

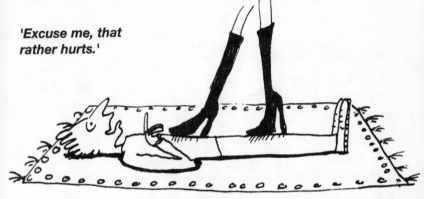

Solution:

The first thing you've got to think about is, why are you so scared to stand up to your mates? They are supposed to be your friends after all, so if they really are that scary, why are you hanging around with them in the first place? If they are good friends it's unlikely that they'll immediately turn on you the moment you confront them about something, so try not to focus on how nasty they may be if you say something (because nine times out of ten they won't be). Instead, work out how to explain why you're fed up, as they may not even have realized that they've done anything to upset you, or if they have, it may be because you have unknowingly done something to upset them too! The key here is communication (or lack of it), and by getting things out in the open (not necessarily arguing) you're more likely to end up with lasting long-term friendships, than if you keep sweeping things under the carpet.

Sometimes it's better to talk.

Sweeping problems under the carpet doesn't help either.

Problem:

Too close for comfort

'I've known my mate Martin since we were five and we've always got on really well, but recently he's been driving me a bit mad. He's always round my house, calling me, or hanging around me at school, which is fine most of the time, but I would like a bit of time to myself, or to spend with other mates. I don't want to tell him to get lost, but I've tried dropping hints for him to back off a bit, and he just isn't getting them. So what do I do now?'

'Well, hello there mate!'

Solution:

It's always going to be hard telling someone you don't want to see them as much, no matter how tactfully you do it and how close you are as mates. However, it's better to be honest with your mates and to try to explain how you feel, rather than bottling it all up and then one day exploding. You don't want to find yourself suddenly yelling that they've become more annoying than a Teletubbie, and twice as dull as dishwater, because trying to rescue a friendship after an outburst like that will take some major negotiations and diplomacy skills. Instead, you should take the initiative and talk to your friend about the situation. You don't have to say that you're sick of the sight of them and never want to see them again.

Action:

Instead sit down together and arrange some specific times when you can both meet up during the week, and if necessary explain that you'll be pretty busy doing other things for the rest of the time. That way your mate can make other plans too and shouldn't feel too let down or neglected.

'Sorry, but according to this you're not my friend on Thursdays.'

Problem:

Caught in the middle

'At school I hang around with a group of mates, but last week two of them had a huge row about some boy, and now they won't talk to each other. I really like them both which is making life very difficult as they both want to slag each other off to me! I wish they'd just sort themselves out, because I'm getting fed up with getting caught in the middle, or being used to pass messages from one to the other. How can I make them friends again so that we can all get back to how we were before?'

'Pass this on to Kelly please.'

Solution:

Ooh, this is a tricky one. The simple answer is that you can't force your mates to patch things up, but you can give them a helping hand. Probably the best way to do this is to get them to agree to spend some time in the same room together, with you acting as an unbiased and impartial observer. Ask each of them to explain to you what their problem is, why they're upset and what they'd like to happen to make them feel better. Once they've taken it in turns to do this, your mates may be surprised to learn how the other one feels, and they might even discover that wires have been crossed somewhere along the way and there really is no reason for them to be cross with each other. If they don't, then it's over to you. Try to get your friends to talk to each other (without shouting, screaming, getting the hump or storming out) in an attempt to reach a compromise. And if all that doesn't work, tell them how upsetting this is for you and your other mates. If they're too proud to apologize to each other, then perhaps they should consider making up in order not to risk losing other friendships.

'Now do you think you can talk to Meg without getting the hump?'

Rachel rescued her friendship.

Problem:

Two's company and three's a crowd

'Andrea and I have been best mates all through infant and then junior school, and now we both go to the same senior school. Throughout all that time the two of us have been so close that some people even think we're sisters. Whatever happens it's always Andrea and Michelle against the world – until recently that is. My problems started at the beginning of last term when a new girl called Tina joined our year. She began hanging out with the two of us which was fine because she can be a real laugh and we all got on pretty well. Then recently Tina began arranging to go out with just Andrea, and neither of them would bother to call me. On Monday at school I'd find out they went shopping together at the weekend, or that Tina fixed up Andrea up with her boyfriend's best mate. It's obvious that Tina would prefer it if I wasn't around, but I can't believe Andrea's dropped me since she came along. How can I rescue our friendship?'

Solution:

You're right to be fed up with your best mate for ditching you like this, and you've also got quite a case against the girl who's done her best to make it happen. It's horrible to suddenly find yourself pushed out onto the sidelines, or replaced by someone new – especially when it's by someone who's only been around five minutes. But before you make any moves you need to work out the following: does your best friend realize how upset you are about all this, and do you think she'd rather replace you with this new person, or be friends with both of you? If she does know what's going on and would happily replace you with this new person, then, frankly you're better off without her. You don't have to go quietly though! Before you look elsewhere for mates worthy of your friendship, try to arrange a time when you can talk to your best mate alone and explain how upset and disappointed you are that she's willing to let go of a friendship as tried and tested as yours for someone who's only just come on the scene.

Talk and make up

If you don't think your best friend really knows what's going on, you've got to have a chat alone with her before things get nasty! Have a few examples of occasions where you've been left out of the friendship up your sleeve, and ask her how she'd feel if this was happening the other way round. If she's any kind of friend, she'll do something about it sharpish – including making sure the two of you spend some quality time alone together like you did in the old days.

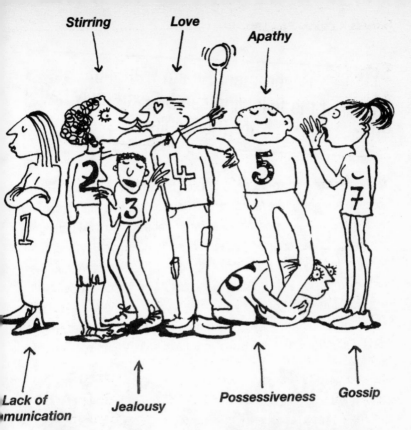

The seven
deadly sins
of friendship

> # Government Health Warning:
> ## All of the following can be extremely bad for friendships

1. Jealousy Envy or rivalry can both be destructive when it comes to even the strongest friendships. The moment you start resenting your friend's looks, possessions, life or abilities, you'll be putting your friendship under enormous strain. Sure, it's OK every now and then to wish you had the same colour hair, or skin as spot-free as theirs, or their dribbling and tackling skills, but if you become obsessed with what they've got and you haven't you're not going to be much fun to be around. So if you become aware that the green-eyed monster is trying to intrude on your friendship, you'd better act fast!

Tell me about it

'My friend has got a PlayStation with loads of fantastic games for it but because my mum doesn't agree with anything to do with guns and fighting, I'm not allowed to play on it, let alone have one of my own. I know I shouldn't but I have to admit that I do get quite jealous of my friend because he seems to have everything I want.'

Karim, 14

'But you can wear it whenever you like.'

2. Possessiveness It may sound a bit weird, but it can be easy for mates to become too close, and that can lead to them smothering their closest friends and driving them away. Like any relationship, things tend to work out better if you can give each other some space and time on your own, and not worry about who's seeing who all the time.

'I've got two best friends, one who I've known for ages and another friend who I met more recently. Because I'm in a different maths group to the two of them they've ended up sitting next to each other and now they've become quite good friends themselves. I know that I should be pleased that they get on, but a part of me is fed up because I feel left out, and they were my friends to start with.'
Miranda, 13

3. Love Heard the one about the amazing disappearing friend? You know the story: boy meets girl, boy and girl fall in love, boy and girl dump their friends so that they can see each other the whole time, boy then dumps girl (or vice versa) and suddenly boy and girl want all their old mates back!! Whether it's you or your mate who's fallen in love, you need to be aware from the start that love and relationships can be destructive to friendships.

'For the last three years, Sarah and I have promised faithfully that we'd never let a boy come between our friendship, and up until recently we'd both stuck to it. Now that she's going out with Gregory I never get to see her and she doesn't even want to chat on the phone for ages like we used to. I've tried pointing this out to her, but she says that I'm just being selfish, and obviously I'm jealous, which is such rubbish.'
Amy, 15

Ruth tried to slip her new boyfriend into the conversation.

'You swear you won't tell a soul?'

4. GOSSIP What may seem like a bit of harmless fun or a laugh can be the biggest enemy to friendship. In the wrong hands gossip can have the best of friends at each other's throats accusing and threatening each other all sorts – even though there really is nothing to be upset about. So the next time someone says to you, 'Don't say that I told you, but my mate's cousin's brother's next-door neighbour reckoned that your mate called you a stupid waste of space who smells of wee,' don't fly off the handle and start an all-out assault on your mate. Remember that it's just gossip, and before you take things any further you should find out the facts.

latest gossip

'Recently I started walking home from school rather than getting picked up by my mum and that's when I met Mikey, a boy who lives nearby and walks the same way. We ended up chatting and he turned out to be really nice and as we had quite a lot in common and got on really well we soon became friends. Unfortunately, that has meant that we now have to put up with loads of gossip being stirred up about us by other people making out that we're more than just mates. It's so stupid and so wrong and it could have ruined the friendship I had with this boy.'

Anna, 15

big mouth

5. Lack of communication

It may make you cringe when your mate insists on humming along to the radio very badly and out of tune, but if you don't tell them that, then what's to stop them carrying on and slowly driving you round the bend? The point is that even the best of friends rarely have telepathic skills, so it's therefore a good idea for you to tell each other stuff like how you feel, what annoys you, why you're upset, what you're up to at the weekend, etc. The more you talk, the less likely you are to misunderstand your friends and fall out with them.

'Is there something up, mate?'

'Whoops, did I hurt your feelings?'

'When me and my friend are mucking about we always call each other stupid names for a laugh but recently I said something that really upset him without realizing it. He was really funny with me after that, and although I was tempted to just ignore him, instead I asked him what was wrong. He said to me, "Why did you call me that name?" He didn't realize that I was just mucking about, and I didn't realize that I'd said something that had upset him. If we hadn't talked about it and explained things to each other we probably wouldn't be friends now.'
David, 13

6. Stirring – as practised by stirrers

You know the type – they thrive on gossip (see deadly sin No. 4) and like nothing better than to see a group of mates arguing about something that they started. If you and your mates value the relationships you have between you, then you should be careful to watch out for when stirrers start butting in and trying to come between you with lies and deceit.

The stirrer.

'I'd always thought that Nicky was a nice girl so when she told me that my best mate Abigail had been spreading it round school that I'd gone all the way with a boy in Year 11, I believed her. I was furious with Abigail and gave her a right mouthful without listening to her side of the story. It was only after I'd calmed down that Abigail promised me she hadn't said anything of the sort and that apparently Nicky had said exactly the same to two other girls in our year. I couldn't believe that someone would deliberately try to wreck our friendship.'
Leanne, 14

7. Apathy The tricky thing about apathy, the final 'friendship deadly sin', is that it can creep up on you without you even noticing. Before you know it, you're taking your mates for granted left, right and centre, then one day you wake up and realize that the people who were once your great mates have drifted away or become 'just people you see around every now and then'. The key to preventing apathy from ruining your friendships is to keep reminding yourself of what a good friend should be and how you're measuring up to that.

'It had taken me all year to get picked for the school football team, so when I finally got selected I trained after school whenever I could. This meant that I saw less and less of my best mate Steven without really realizing it – I was so wrapped up with the football. It was only when I was dropped from the team the next term I realized how stupid I'd been to ignore him for all that time – when I called him to see if he could come out, his mum told me that he was out with his new mates.' **George, 14**

'Now where did Fred get to?'

How to steer clear of trouble

So, if those are the seven deadly sins, how do you make sure they don't ruin your friendships? Easy: you **KEEP TALKING** to your mates about everything, and **DON'T EVER PRESUME** that you know what they're thinking, or that they know what you're thinking. At the same time, although you should always be prepared to **MAKE THE EFFORT** for your mates, you should also be confident enough to **GIVE THEM SOME SPACE**. Before you jump down you friend's throat because of something you've heard they've said or done, remember to **BEWARE OF STIRRERS** who try to interfere, gossip or stir things up, and **FIND OUT THE FACTS** before you leap to any conclusions or make any accusations. Finally, and perhaps most importantly of all, **DON'T TAKE THEM FOR GRANTED**, because if you do, you could find they're not there for you when you most need them.

'Can we talk about this?'

A friend in need

You know how to have a laugh and share the good times with your friends, but can you tell when things aren't going well for them, and would you know what to do if they weren't?

'It's just that nobody listens to me...'

You may think it's easy to tell when someone's feeling down or depressed, but it's often the people you're closest to who are the last to realize that you've got a problem. So before you presume that everything's fine with your mates, take a look at the following quiz to see if you really know what's on your mind or theirs.

'Come on, it's not that bad!'

Quiz

Could You Spot A Mate In Trouble?

The statements in section one apply to female friends, and the statements in section two (Numbers. 11-20) are for male friends. Get a piece of paper and count up how many of the following apply to you.

Section 1

- The main subjects I talk about with my best friend are clothes, music, movies, boys and boys!
- It freaks me out when she goes all quiet and reserved
- It gets on my nerves when she's stroppy and moody for no reason
- If she doesn't want to go out and do things with me, I just leave her alone
- Sometimes when I ask her if there's anything wrong, she won't answer one way or the other
- I've never seen my mate cry
- I don't understand why she sometimes doesn't return my calls
- I can't keep up with her moods – one minute she'll be fine and the next she's depressed and miserable
- It sometimes seems that I can't do anything right as far as she's concerned
- I don't get too involved in her relationships or family life – that's her business

Section 2

- The main subjects my best mate and I talk about are music, girls, footie and footie!
- I don't understand why he gets so moody at times
- It gets on my nerves when he gets the hump for no reason
- If he doesn't want to hang out or kick around with me, I just leave him alone
- Sometimes if I ask him if there's anything wrong, he just shrugs and won't answer one way or the other

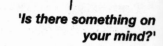

'Is there something on your mind?'

- I've never seen my mate get really angry or upset
- I don't understand why he sometimes doesn't call me back when I've phoned him
- It's really confusing when he seems OK one minute and the next he's depressed and miserable
- It sometimes seems as though I can't do anything right as far as he's concerned
- I don't get too involved in his relationships or family life

'Nothing personal mate, but don't bring your private life onto the pitch – OK?'

How did you rate?

If you found that more than five of the statements in each section applied to you, that's a pretty good indication that your mate is worried or upset about something and that you haven't picked up on the signals they're sending out – you klutz! OK, so they may not have told you 'in words' that something's wrong or that they'd like help, but that shouldn't stop you offering a sympathetic ear and some advice. Just because you may have been able to sort out your own problems in the past, it doesn't mean everyone else can get by without help or support. Naturally this won't be a bundle of laughs, and it can be hard work being around someone who's miserable, but unless you're prepared to sit down and listen to what they have to say, this friendship won't go the distance. But, don't panic  and don't worry about not having a GCSE in Advanced Psychotherapy and Friendship Counselling, sometimes just being there for a friend is enough. You don't have to come up with any magic solutions, or land yourself with any major chores. All he or she probably needs is someone to listen to their problems. If any of your friends are worried about lumbering you with their worries, it doesn't hurt to remind them that this is exactly the kind of thing friends are for. Often this is all a mate needs to get them through a tough time.

Tell me about it

'A friend of mine got behind with her school work recently and was sent to the headmistress. She was really worried about it, so I made sure I was there before and after to comfort her and check that she was OK.' **Gemma, 13**

'I had a friend who I'd known since I was one and when we went to senior school we ended up in different classes. Because he's only little, he ended up getting picked on. Whenever that happened he'd always come to me for help and I'd always stick up for him, even if the other boys were bigger than me.' **Jake, 12**

'One of my friends was really struggling with her homework, so I'd lend her my work and help her with hers until she got the hang of it.' **Rozina, 13**

'I was being picked on at school by these other girls and I was too scared to do anything about it, but my best friend stuck up for me and helped me sort it out.' **Alice, 13**

'My best mate's big brother is really horrible to him, and one day he came into school with a big scratch on his face. He was really scared to tell anyone but when I asked him about it he told me what had happened. I told him he shouldn't have to take that and said I'd help him out if I could. Since then he's become a bit more confident and whereas he used to be really shy, now he's trying to get involved in more things.'
James, 12

Jack's new friend really helped boost his confidence.

I'll be there for you

I f you think your friend is in trouble or depressed, don't ignore the fact and hope that it will go away – find out if you can help. But before you go steaming in armed with your box of hankies demanding that they spill their guts Jerry Springer style, you need to have a plan of action. Luckily, here's one we prepared earlier.

The seven steps to helping a friend in need

1. Let them know you've noticed something is wrong

2. Don't be too pushy or demanding about them telling you what the problem is

3. Know when to back off and give them some space and time to think about things

4. When the time is right, gently encourage them to talk and tell you what the problem is

5. If they don't want to talk at that moment, tell them that you'll always be there to listen if they need you

6. Ask if there is anyone else they would like to talk to

7. Whatever their problem turns out to be, take it seriously even if it seems trivial to you, but at the same time help them to keep a sense of proportion

'I'm sure he's gone to mousey heaven.'

Alarm bells

Once in a while you might be so worried about a friend that you may need advice from someone else on what to do. This doesn't mean posting a notice in the school assembly hall asking for any suggestions, or discussing their problems with other members of the bus queue. If your mate has asked you to keep their problem a secret then it's your duty to do just that unless of course you feel that things are getting out of hand and it's a really serious issue. That's when you may have to look elsewhere for help. If your friend confides in you that he or she is worried about any of the following danger zones, alarm bells should ring and that's when you seriously need to think about getting some back-up:

- **underage sex, contraception or pregnancy scares**
- **physical, sexual or mental abuse**
- **eating disorders or other health worries**
- **bullying**
- **racism**

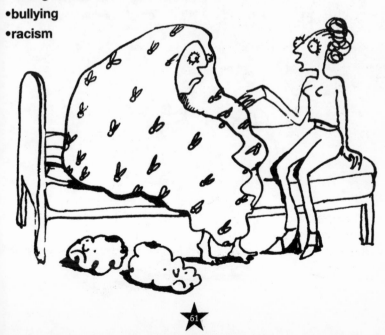

You can get support and extra help for any of the above problems from all sorts of different sources, so don't panic, just think about approaching one or more of the following:

- **understanding parents, aunts, uncles, grandparents or friends' parents and families**
- **sympathetic teachers or year heads**
- **recognized help lines or organizations – see page 94 for a list of relevant addresses and phone numbers**
- **a nurse or doctor at your local surgery**

The best thing you can do as a true friend is to encourage your mate to get that help. And remember, there are circumstances when you alone really can't do any more to help and there are times when not involving someone else might put you or your friend in danger. Looking elsewhere for help doesn't make you a hopeless mate, and you won't have let your friend down – quite the opposite. You're putting their welfare first, and that's the sign of true friendship.

Helping friends to help themselves

When friends are in trouble or upset and worried about something, it can be tempting to wade in and try to make everything better for them. But wait a minute: is it your job to sort out all of your friends' problems, or are there ways of helping them do it for themselves? Now we're really getting on to 'Advanced Friendship Techniques' (AFT), but in the long term, this can be a much better plan of action. It helps your friends to stand on their own two feet, gives them a sense of independence and self-confidence, and this in turn will make them much better mates to hang out with. Up for it? Then take a look at the six-point 'AFT' plan to helping a friend in need.

1 The first step to helping your friends is by listening to them – and that means really listening. This can be harder than you think. Don't believe it? OK then, try experimenting by sitting down with a friend one-to-one and timing yourself listening to him/her talk for 1–2 minutes without saying anything or interrupting. Harder than you thought, isn't it?

The art of listening.

'Aaaaaaahahh ... I know exactly how you feel.'

2 Once you've listened to your friend's problem, you could give them advice by referring to things you have done or experienced in the past that have worked for you. This can be helpful, but sometimes all it amounts to is you telling them what to do, and remember, what worked for you may not work for them. Instead, if you ask the right questions, people usually find they have the answers, so try asking things like, 'What is it you want to do?' or 'Who do you want to talk to first?'

3 Bear in mind that however close the two of you are, and however well you think you know someone, at the end of the day everyone's different and feels or experiences things differently, so don't say 'I know exactly how you feel'. How can you?

4 Encourage your friend to talk and share their worries with you – tell them they are doing the right thing in talking, because a problem shared is a problem halved.

5 You can give support in other ways. Just by being with them when they need you or standing by them when times are tough, for example, if other people are giving them a hard time.

6 Find out if there is any information that may help your friend, for example information on bullying, and offer to go with them if they need help in talking to someone else about their problem.

Stand by your friends.

Helping yourself

Sometimes it can be tough being a friend to someone with major problems. By taking on their worries, you're automatically lumbering yourself too, and if it's you who's doing all the listening and understanding, who's there to help you? Being there when horrible things are happening to your friends, for example seeing them get hit by a parent, or become the victim of a racist attack, can be an incredibly tough thing to deal with, and it wouldn't be wrong of you to want some support for yourself.

Confiding in someone who can help you isn't the same thing as betraying your friend's trust by gossiping about the situation to other friends. If the pressure of your friends' problems is making you depressed and upset you won't be much use to them, so get some help from one or more of the following people:

- an older brother or sister
- parents
- an understanding teacher
- someone independent like a school counsellor
- ChildLine, or one of the other help lines listed at the back of the book (page 94–96)

Latest gossip.

Real-life friends in action

M
ost of the time friends are there to have a laugh with, but sometimes they'll be there for a whole lot more.

Highs and lows `True Story`

'Rebecca was used to me moaning about my parents arguing, because that's what they seemed to do most of the time. It got so bad that I'd avoid going home whenever I could, and I don't think there was ever a time when Becs didn't say, "Why don't you have tea round my house?". That was how things stayed for almost a year, until one day when I got home from school to find my mum in tears in the kitchen and dad gone. He'd met someone else and wanted to be with her, so that left just me and mum. Throughout the next few months I had to deal with my dad not being there. Even though he'd let us both down, I did miss him loads and I couldn't get used to the idea that my parents were going to get divorced.

divorced

A great listener

'I think I would have gone completely mad if it hadn't been for Rebecca. She was always there for me and was pretty much the only person I could talk to about it – as soon as I tried to bring it up with mum she'd either shout at me to stop talking about "That bastard" or burst into tears. There were loads of nights when I'd escape to Rebecca's house. We'd sit in her room and I'd pour my heart out to her. In fact in those first few weeks I told her all sorts of really personal family stuff that no one else knew. It must have driven her mad at times, but that never stopped her from inviting me round or being on the end of the phone. She'd just listen and offer advice when she could. Looking back, I think the most amazing thing about it all was that she didn't say a word about any of my problems to anyone else at school – and there was some really juicy stuff that would have made excellent gossip.'

I'll never forget what she did for me, and I'll never be able to thank her enough.'
Lucy, 15

Boys don't cry True Story

'I'd always been really close to my Uncle Tom. He was quite a lot younger than his brother, my dad, and so he was a bit easier to talk to about stuff and always a right laugh with it. He used to take me to see Villa for practically every home game, and when mum and dad were getting on my nerves I'd go round to his house where we could talk about footie and music and stuff. He was into Pulp and The Verve – bands my parents didn't have a clue about – and when I was round at his house I could play my CDs really loud and instead of yelling at me to turn it down, he'd usually sing along – very badly.

All my mates liked him too, especially Darren, my best mate, who used to come with me to Uncle Tom's to hang out. Darren would always say how lucky I was to have an Uncle Tom, but I didn't really need reminding, because I knew that for myself.

'I'm a lucky mannnn...'

Tragedy

'It was in the summer of last year that Tom died. He was on his motorbike on a motorway and there was an accident. Mum and dad wouldn't really tell me much about it because they didn't want to upset me. But one minute he was there and the next he wasn't. We were supposed to be seeing Villa play Arsenal on the Saturday of his funeral. Mum and dad didn't want me to go to the funeral, but I told them they couldn't stop me. To prove that it wouldn't get to me I made sure I didn't cry in front of them – or anyone. In fact I didn't really let anyone know how I felt, even though inside I felt like dying myself.

So alone

'I missed Tom so much, but that's not the sort of thing a bloke can say out loud without everyone taking the mickey out of him. Except Darren. After Tom died I didn't really leave the house much except to go to school, and I wouldn't talk to anyone on the phone when they called. I'd just get mum to say I was in the bath or out. Soon my mates stopped calling – except Darren. He kept coming round and trying to get me out even though I'd always say no. Then about three weeks after the funeral he came round to see if I wanted to go down the rec and have a kick about. I was about to say "No thanks" again when he said, "Well, I'll just come in for a session of *Metal Gear Solid* then". Before I had the chance to say anything, he was on his way up to my room.

Letting go

'When I got up there, he had put The Verve album on and was setting up the PlayStation. I hadn't really listened to the album since Tom had died, and just as I was thinking that Darren said, "Do you miss him then?". It was almost as if he'd read my mind. That's when I started crying. I couldn't believe I was doing it in front of another bloke. Shame. But instead of laughing or taking the mick, Darren just got me some loo roll to blow my nose on. It was the first time I'd been able to cry, or get upset or talk about Tom since he'd gone. At first it felt awful, but after twenty minutes or so, believe it or not, we were laughing. Darren had remembered how Tom used to do a brilliant *Men Behaving Badly* dance, then I remembered how bad his singing was. For the next hour I talked to Darren about Tom, how much I missed him, and how bad the last month had been.

True Friendship

'Darren didn't really offer any advice, or say anything much, but he did just listen and somehow that made me feel better. And the even more amazing thing was that Darren didn't ever tell anyone about how I'd cried, or take the mick out of me about what had happened in my room that afternoon. We don't talk about it much now, but I know that if I did need to get something out in the open, I could talk to Darren about it.'

'I'll never ever forget Uncle Tom, or stop missing him, but after that day when Darren came round, I did start to get on with my life, and I realized that although I didn't have a brilliant uncle any more, I did have a fantastic best mate.'
Steven, 14,

Brilliant

True Story

Partners in dieting

'Karen and I started our diets on the same day. We didn't tell our mums because they would have gone mad, but we'd both decided that we were getting a bit podgy and so decided to lose some weight. Two weeks later and I hadn't lost any weight, but I was totally fed up with avoiding chips and lying to my mum about what I had (or hadn't) had for lunch. Karen, on the other hand, was on a mission. I don't know how she did it, but there were days when she wouldn't eat anything other than an apple or a cream cracker. She started to lose weight and at first I was really impressed by her self-discipline and determination. Then, I have to confess, I was a bit jealous because everyone was commenting on how good she looked now that she'd lost some weight, and boys were starting to take a bit more interest.

'A couple of months later and Karen was still totally obsessed with losing weight, even though she was looking pretty thin by now – almost too thin. When I tried to talk to her about it, she'd get really funny and try to change the subject. It got boring when we'd go down the town and I'd suggest going to McDonalds and she'd either say no, or go begrudgingly and just have a Diet Coke.

Close to the edge

'I realized that she was taking her diet too far when she began to get really funny about us getting ready together to go out. She wouldn't get changed in front of me, and would get stroppy and defensive if I told her she looked great. Even though by now she was tiny she'd insist that she looked fat and ugly. She just didn't seem like her normal carefree self any more, and there was certainly no more pigging out on a huge bar of Galaxy over a video together. I tried talking to her about it, and suggested that she should forget dieting, but she didn't want to listen.

'It really upset me to watch her making herself ill – she'd get tired and listless and couldn't concentrate at school. It took me ages to pluck up the courage to talk to someone else about it – I felt like I was betraying her – but I couldn't sit back and watch her get worse. Eventually I went to see our school counsellor. She was really understanding, and assured me that I'd done the right thing, but when Karen found out I wasn't so sure. She went mental when she found out what I'd done. She wouldn't talk to me and refused to see me, and that was really hard. I was so upset and worried that I'd done the wrong thing – I'd lost my best friend, and it looked like there was nothing I could do to get her back. I'd just about given up hope of Karen ever talking to me again when I got a call from her. She'd been seeing a specialist eating disorders counsellor and although she'd said it was really tough at first, things were starting to get better for her. She realized that the dieting was taking over her life and was a serious problem, and now that she was learning how to deal with it, she wanted to thank me for what I'd done.'

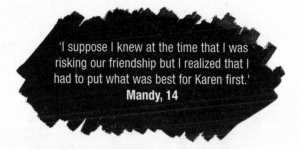

'I suppose I knew at the time that I was risking our friendship but I realized that I had to put what was best for Karen first.'
Mandy, 14

opposites
attract

Remember when you were at primary school, and friends were just friends? There wasn't really such a thing as 'boyfriends' or 'girlfriends', you all just got on with it (with the exception of a quick game of kiss chase every now and then, which frankly you'd rather forget about now). From about the age of about 11, however, things may start to change. As well as getting on as mates with the opposite sex, there's a chance you may end up fancying some of them. Nothing wrong with that, in fact it can be rather nice, but it doesn't mean that you should suddenly start thinking of them all just as objects of desire.

Good reasons to be just good friends

1 You get to understand how 'the other half' think. This can be extremely useful if you're having trouble with a boyfriend or girlfriend, or you're just finding it difficult to suss out someone you fancy. A friend who's a member of the opposite sex may well be able to give you some invaluable 'insider' secrets.

2 If you're hanging out with members of the opposite sex as mates, then it's much more likely that you'll be more relaxed in their company when you do start dating.

3 You get to see things from another point of view. Let's face it, however much we'd like to think that there shouldn't be any differences between boys and girls, they're out there and the more we understand each other, the less likely it is that we'll come up against misunderstandings.

Tell me about it

'I seem to be able to talk to my friend who's a boy more than my girl friends, but I think that's just because I've known him for so long and we've been through quite a lot together. It wouldn't matter if he was a boy or a girl, we'd still get on just the same.' **Lily, 15**

'Does my bum look big in this?'

Tell me about it

'At my last school I was really close to a girl in my year, but just as a friend, not as a girlfriend. It turned out that she really liked my best mate a lot and I already knew that he liked her but because they were both really shy they wouldn't talk to each other. Instead they'd tell me what to say to the other one and I ended up running back and forwards between the two of them. I didn't mind though because they were both my mates and I thought it was pretty cool that they wanted to go out with each other.' **Callum, 14**

'Abby asked me to ask you to hold hands with her.'

I haven't
got any
friends

There may be times when you feel as though you haven't got a friend in the world, or perhaps the friends you've got suddenly turn against you. If this happens to you, regardless of why it happened or whose fault it was, there's one thing for certain – you're going to feel pretty cut up.

Tell me about it

'I've just been dumped by my mates, but my older cousin told me that when she was my age she fell out with her friends a lot too, and it made her feel as though she didn't want to go to school.' **Joanne, 13**

'If you've fallen out with your friends and you're left out of the group it can be really horrible because you feel as though they're talking about you all the time and getting other people to talk about you too.' **Debbie, 12**

Debbie didn't know if she was being left out or not.

There's often a lot of pressure on you to feel 'popular' and to be surrounded by acres of mates who all think you're great, and if that isn't the case it's inevitable that you'll begin to wonder if there's something wrong with you. There's no easy answer to this problem. You can't force people to be your friends and you can't buy friendship, but if you make sure you're true to yourself, and that you're the person you want to be, then you're far more likely to attract friends on your wavelength. It can be tempting to start acting in a certain way or wearing certain clothes that you may not feel comfortable with, but feel will make you appear a better potential friend. Big mistake. How long can you keep up that act? And anyway, why would you want to 'pretend' to be

At last Billy had the ultimate fashion accessory for making new friends.

something you're not just to attract mates who aren't your type?

'If you try to be a certain kind of person just to make new friends that can get you into trouble, because you may end up knowing them for years and years and you wouldn't be able to keep up an act for that long. You'd get found out sooner and later.' **Megan, 14**

What went wrong?

If you've suddenly been dumped by your friend (or friends), it might be worth trying to get to the bottom of what's happened – remember the Seven Deadly Sins of Friendship? It's possible that numbers 1, 2, 4, 5 and 6 (i.e. jealousy, possessiveness, gossip, lack of communication and stirring) have gone and done the dirty. If you can find out exactly what's happened, then there's a chance that you could talk through the problems and rescue your friendship. Sure, it might seem as though it would be easier just to walk away, but if you're prepared to make the effort to sort things out, you'll probably end up with an even stronger friendship than before.

I think we should talk.

sorted

Quiz: How well do you really know your best mate?

Do you and your best mate know each other inside out? Or are you just a couple of people who happen to live in the same street, or go to the same school? Find out by grabbing a pen and a piece of paper each, then sit down with your mate and read out the following questions one at a time. Both write down your answers on separate pieces of paper, without the other one seeing – and no conferring!! Once you have finished, swap pieces of paper and refer back to the questions to see how much you've got right about each other.

1. Who would he/she most like to snog in the world?
2. What football team does he/she support? (One bonus point if you can name their favourite player in the team)
3. Has he/she got any posters on his/her bedroom walls? (One bonus point if you can say who or what the posters are of)
4. What was the last record he/she bought?
5. What would he/she most like to eat for dinner tonight?

6. What is his/her favourite item of clothing?

7. Who does he/she fancy at the moment?

8. Who was the first person he/she ever fancied?

9. Where would his/her ideal first date be?

10. What's his/her biggest secret?

11. What does he/she want to do when he/she leaves school?

12. What telly programme(s) would he/she rather die than miss?

'She must have a secret in here somewhere.'

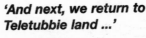

'And next, we return to Teletubbie land ...'

If you scored: 0-3

Oh dear, do you ever really talk or listen to your mates, or are they just hanging around in the background like wallpaper? Friendship doesn't necessarily mean knowing absolutely everything about each other, but by the sounds of it, you'd be hard pushed to remember his/her phone number! A score this low usually indicates one of two things:

1 You're the one who tends to do all the talking (and not much listening) when it comes to your friendships, and so although your mate(s) may know a fair bit about you, you're pretty much in the dark when it comes to their lives. OK, so this may suit you just fine, but don't expect your friends to hang around too long. After all, what's in it for them?

2 Although you like hanging out with your mates, you also like keeping your cards close to your chest and your friends at arm's length. This may be because you don't want to be let down,

'I'm sure I had a friend around here somewhere?'

so you make sure you don't rely on anyone, or you feel that your life is your business, and the same applies to them. Fair enough, but you don't have to reveal all your innermost secrets in order to get to know someone better and develop a great friendship.

So, if you think it's because of No.1 you might want to try taking the time to listen to your mates a bit more and keeping your trap shut for more than five minutes. If it's because of No.2, lighten up a little! Revealing a little bit more of what you're about to trustworthy, understanding friends could mean that they'll be there for you when you need them in the future because they'll understand a bit more what makes you tick.

4-8

It looks like this friendship is coming along nicely, so don't be too hard on yourselves if you didn't get absolutely everything about each other right. And if this quiz has got you both talking about

'So does this make you angry? upset? annoyed? scared? or a mixture?'

stuff, why not use the opportunity to make a note of the gaps in your friendship – whether it's general knowledge about each other's lives, or slightly deeper stuff about what makes you angry, upset, annoyed or scared. Sometimes it's too easy to get caught up in the trivia of everyday life, and you forget to really talk about things that are getting to you, and if you can't talk to your mates about it, who can you talk to?

9–12

Well, isn't it a shame that there isn't a GCSE in 'Friendship and the lives of best friends'? Because if there were, you'd certainly be well on the way to getting an 'A'. By getting such a high score, it shows that your friendships really are two-way relationships that you take pretty seriously.

Either that or you've been:

- **cheating**
- **rifling through your mate's top secret diary**
- **or secretly developing psychic powers**

If it's any of the above, go to the back of the class, hang your head in shame and start to take your friendships seriously.

The Friendship Charter

The friends you have now will probably be the ones you remember for the rest of your life – whether or not you make it past the school leaving hurdle and stay in touch – so make the very most of them while you can. To ensure you're being the best kind of friend you can, there are certain guidelines you should stick to as a mate – you could call it 'the friendship charter' – and paying attention to this 'charter' or ignoring it could make all the difference to your friendships. Remember, helping a friend in need can be one of the most rewarding things you ever do to .But, at the same time, letting down a friend can be one of the most devastating things you ever do. If you want to take your friendships seriously, you should get together with your mates and all agree to stick by the following:

I, **MR OR MRS TOP MATE**, promise to:

- always be there for my mates when they need me
- never let my mates down by gossiping or telling their secrets
- think carefully about what's best for my mates, and get them the help they need when they need it

HELP!

If you or a friend need help, but you don't know where to turn, your first step could be to contact ChildLine (see below). All calls are confidential, you don't have to tell them your name, and the phone call is free. If you or a friend have a more specific problem, the phone numbers below may also be of help.

General

ChildLine: Freepost 1111 London N1 OBR
24-hr helpline: 0800 1111
Children's Legal Centre 01206 873 820
Depression Alliance 0171 633 9929
Eating Disorders Association 01603 619 090
eda@netcom.co.uk
Health Information Service They can refer you to a relevant organization for your problem and publish lots of useful information on a whole range of health issues. Tel: 0800 66 55 44
Overeaters Anonymous 24-hr information line: 0700 784 985
Samaritans 0345 90 90 90
The Acne Support Group 0181 561 6868
Young People's Information Centre Advice on a range of subjects. Tel: 01707 266223
Youth Access Will refer you to a local youth counselling service. Tel: 0181 772 9900

Alcohol and drugs

Alanon 24-hr helpline for families and friends of problem drinkers. Tel: 0171 403 0888
National Drugs Helpline 0800 77 66 00

Contraception, pregnancy and sexual health

British Pregnancy Advisory Service Action Line 0345 304 030

Brook Advisory Centres 0171 713 9000 (Mon–Fri, 9am–5pm)

Family Planning Association 0171 837 4044

Contraceptive Education Service England: 0171 837 4044;
Scotland: 0141 576 5088; Wales: 01222 342 766;
N Ireland: 01232 325488

Violence and sexual abuse

Anti-Bullying Campaign 0171 378 1446

anti-bullying@compuserve.com

NSPCC Child Protection 0800 800 500

Rape and Sexual Abuse Support Line 01923 241 600

Families

National Family Mediation 0171 383 5993

general@nfn.org.uk

Gingerbread Advice for single parent families. Helpline: 0171 336 8184

National Society for the Prevention of Cruelty to Children (NSPCC) 24-hr child protection helpline: 0800 800 500

Lifestyle and sexuality

London Lesbian and Gay Switchboard 24-hr national helpline:
0171 837 7324/4238

The Vegetarian Society 0161 928 0793

Bereavement

Cruse Youth Line 0181 940 3131

Child Death Helpline 0800 282 986 (Mon, Wed, Fri, 10am–1pm; daily, 7–10pm)

Homelessness and runaways

Missing Persons Helpline 0500 700 700
Message Home Service Freecall 0500 700 740
Shelter 0171 505 2000

Books to read

Am I Normal? Anita Naik (Hodder, 1997)
Boys about Boys: The facts, fears and fantasies by Nick Fisher (Macmillan, 1998)
Dealing with Stress by Emma Haughton (Wayland, 1995)
Face the Facts: Sex and Relationships by Jillian Powell (Wayland, 1997)
Friends or Enemies? by Anita Naik
(Hodder Children's Books, 1998)
I was a Teenage Worrier by Ros Asquith ((Corgi, 1992)
Respect Yourself! Be Your Own Best
(Hodder Children's Books, 1998)
Say What You Mean and
Get What You Want
by Tricia Kreitman (Macmillan, 1998)
Young Citizen: Growing Up
by Kate Brookes (Wayland, 1999)